Watching the Weather

Thunder and Lightning

Elizabeth Miles

Heinemann Library
Chicago, Illinois

Customer Service 888-454-2279
Visit our website at www.heinemannlibrary.com

Designed by Richard Parker and Celia Jones
Illustrations by Jeff Edwards
Originated by Dot Gradations
Printed and bound in China by South China Printing Company

09 08 07 06 05
10 9 8 7 6 5 4 3 2 1

Library of Congress Cataloging-in-Publication Data

Miles, Elizabeth, 1960-
   Thunder and lightning / Elizabeth Miles.
      p. cm. -- (Watching the weather)
Includes bibliographical references and index.
ISBN 1-4034-5579-1 (HC), 1-4034-5677-1 (Pbk.)
1. Thunder--Juvenile literature. 2. Lightning--Juvenile literature. I. Title. II. Series.
QC968.2.M55 2005
551.55'4--dc22

                          2004002374

Acknowledgments

The author and publisher are grateful to the following for permission to reproduce copyright material: Corbis/Jose Luis Pelaez, Inc. p. 5; Corbis/Ray Bird p. 22; Corbis/Raymond Gehman p. 17; Corbis/RF pp. 4, 10; Corbis/Roger Ressmeyer p. 26; Corbis/Tom Bean p. 14; FLPA p. 25; Getty images/Digital Vision p. 6; Getty Images/Photodisc pp. I, 11; Getty/Image Bank p. 16; Harcourt Education Ltd/Tudor photography pp. 28, 29; Rex features/Kim Ludbrook p. 27; Science Photo Library/George Post p. 9; SPL/Munoz-Yague/Eurelios p. 18; SPL/Jim Reed pp. 20, 21; SPL/Keith Kent pp. 12, 15; SPL/Pekka Parviainen p. 8; SPL/Peter Menzel p. 19; Zefa p. 13.

Cover photograph of lightning over Tuscon, reproduced with permission of Corbis/Tom Ives.

Every effort has been made to contact copyright holders of any material reproduced in this book. Any omissions will be rectified in subsequent printings if notice is given to the publisher.

Contents

Some words are shown in bold, **like this**. You can find out what they mean by looking in the glossary.

What Is a Thunderstorm?

A thunderstorm is a storm with flashes of lightning and claps of thunder. It brings tall, dark clouds.

A thunderstorm can last for a few minutes or many hours.

The rain that falls during a thunderstorm can make you very wet, very quickly!

Everyone runs for cover when a thunderstorm begins. Thunderstorms often bring a lot of rain and sometimes even **hail**.

What Is Lightning?

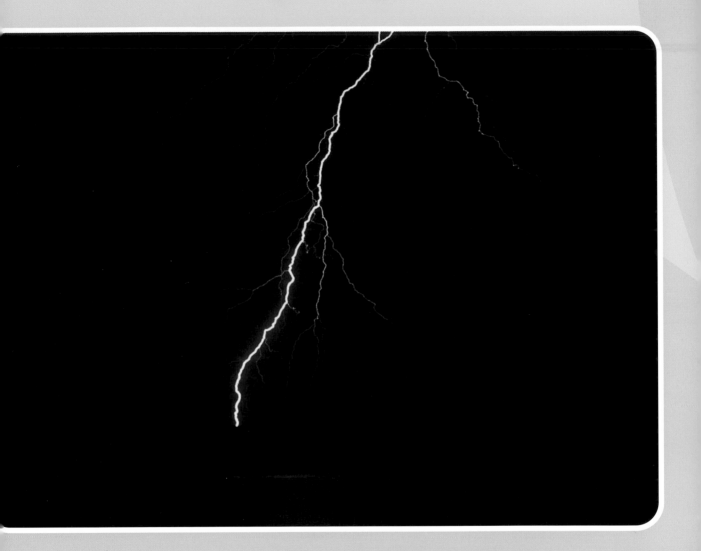

Lightning is a flash of light in the sky. A lightning flash can happen in less than a second. If you blink, you might miss it!

Lightning can jump from cloud to cloud.
Sometimes it jumps from a cloud to the
ground. It can also hit trees and houses.

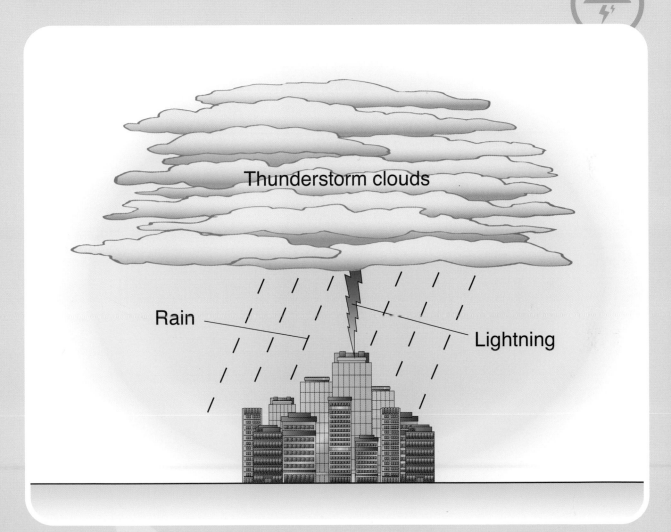

Thunderstorm clouds

Rain

Lightning

What Causes Lightning?

Electricity causes lightning. There is electricity in thunderstorm clouds. Sometimes this electricity causes giant sparks of hot light. These are flashes of lightning.

The electricity that causes lightning comes from storm clouds such as this one.

Lightning is very bright because it is very hot. A flash of lightning is about five times hotter than the surface of the Sun.

What Is Thunder?

Thunder is the noise you can hear in a thunderstorm. Lightning sparks heat the air so quickly that it **explodes**. This makes the clap of thunder.

Thunder happens at the same time as lightning, but we see the lightning before we hear the thunder. This is because light travels through air faster than sound.

Thunder can be very loud if you are close to the storm.

Lightning Shapes

Lightning takes different shapes. Forked lightning splits into branches. It can come down from the cloud to the ground. It can also go across the sky to another cloud.

This forked lightning is jumping from cloud to cloud.

Sheet lightning looks like a brilliant white light.

When a lightning flash is hidden behind a cloud, it is called sheet lightning. The cloud hides the lines of the flash, so we mostly see a glow.

Thunderstorms and Animals

If lightning hits sheep in a field, it can kill them.

Thunderstorms can be dangerous. It does not happen very often, but lightning can kill animals in fields.

Lightning can even kill fish in a lake. This is because **electricity** can spread far through water.

Lightning can jump from clouds to a lake, like in this picture.

Lightning and Plants

Lightning often strikes tall things, such as trees. It is dangerous to stand under a tree during a storm. If the tree is struck by lightning, you might get hurt, too.

Lightning can set fire to a tree. If the tree is in a forest, other trees can catch fire, too. In hot summers, lightning can start huge **forest fires**.

After lightning has struck, a whole forest can be badly damaged.

Flying Through a Storm

Some special planes fly through storm clouds. People inside take measurements to learn more about thunderstorms. Then they send this information to **meteorologists**.

This plane is very strong. It will not be damaged if it is struck by lightning.

A storm cloud shows up
red and yellow on a
pilot's screen.

Ordinary planes have equipment that
can tell if a thunderstorm is close.
If **pilots** know a storm is ahead, they
can fly around it.

Storm Warnings

Weather stations have many instruments. These measure things such as air **temperature** and wind speed.

Meteorologists can tell us if a thunderstorm is on its way. They figure out what the weather will be like by looking at different measurements.

Thunderstorms can form on hot, sticky days. Warm air rises from the ground. If the air rises very quickly, meteorologists know a thunderstorm might form.

Dark storm clouds cover the sky before a thunderstorm.

Staying Safe: People

This tree was struck by lightning. Never stand under a tree during a thunderstorm.

Very few people are struck by lightning, but lightning can kill. In a thunderstorm, do not take any risks. You should go inside a building if you can.

Safety code

Follow these rules to be safe in a thunderstorm.

Things to do	Things not to do
• Get into a building or a car. Shut all doors and windows. • If you are in or near water, get away fast. • If there is no shelter, lie on the ground face down. • Keep away from metal or electrical things such as telephones.	• Never stand near trees, telephone poles, or under an umbrella. • Do not sit on a hill. Run down to the bottom.

Staying Safe: Buildings

Lightning can damage buildings and start fires. People put **lightning rods** on the tops of tall buildings. This keeps the buildings safe.

If lightning strikes, it hits the rod, not the building. A wire carries it down to the ground, away from the building.

Lightning conductor

Wire

If a building is struck by lightning, things inside can be damaged. Computers, televisions, and telephones should be unplugged during a thunderstorm to keep them safe.

Lightning rods need to be placed high up on buildings to keep the buildings safe from thunderstorms.

Disaster: Lightning Strikes

When lightning strikes land, it spreads like ripples in a pond. It can spread across a playing field and hurt several people at the same time.

Lightning strikes Earth many times every day.

If lightning strikes, buildings can catch fire.

Lightning can ruin buildings and burn trees because it is hot and powerful. It heats bricks and trees so quickly that they can **explode**.

Project: Making Electricity

Electricity causes lightning. Try making your own electricity at home.

You will need:
• a balloon

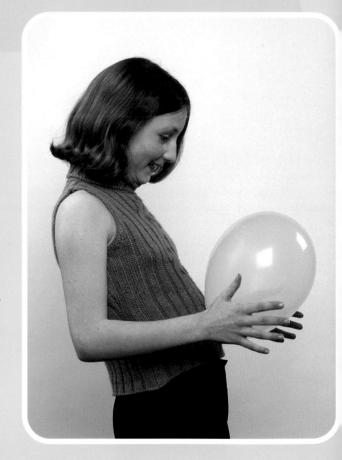

1. Blow up the balloon and tie it.

2. Rub the balloon against your sweater or T-shirt.

3. Hold the balloon against your clothes, a wall, or the ceiling. What happens? The balloon should stick.

4. You can also try rubbing the balloon against your hair.

5. Then hold the balloon away from your hair.

What happens?
Rubbing the balloon on your sweater or your hair gives it an **electrical charge**. This is a little bit like the electrical charge in a thunderstorm cloud. This charge makes the balloon stick to your clothes. It also pulls your hair toward the balloon.

Glossary

electrical charge force that is caused by electricity

electricity kind of energy. Many lights and machines need electricity to make them work.

explode burst apart

forest fire fire that burns down large areas of forest

hail pebble-shaped pieces of ice that fall from clouds

lightning rod metal piece fixed on a building that picks up the electricity from a lightning strike and takes it to the ground

meteorologist person who figures out what the weather is going to be like

pilot person who flies a plane

temperature measure of how hot or cold things are

weather station place where weather measurements are taken and recorded

More Books to Read

Ashwell, Miranda and Andy Owen. *Watching the Weather*. Chicago: Heinemann Library, 1999.

Chambers, Catherine. *Thunderstorm*. Chicago: Heinemann Library, 2003.

Doudna, Kelly. *It Is Stormy*. Edina, Minn.: ABDO Publishing Company, 2003.

Flanagan, Alice. *Lightning*. Eden Prairie, Minn.: The Child's World, 2003.

Sherman, Joseph. *A Book About Lightning*. Minneapolis: Picture Window Books, 2004.

Index